# Mother of Flip-Flops

Mukahang Limbu

**Out-Spoken Press**
London

Published by Out-Spoken Press,
Unit 39, Containerville
1 Emma Street
London, E2 9FP

A CIP record for this title is available from the British Library.

First edition published 2022
ISBN: 978-1-8384272-8-3

Typeset in Adobe Caslon
Design by Patricia Ferguson
Printed and bound by Print Resources

Out-Spoken Press is supported using public funding by the National
Lottery through Arts Council England.

'Dear Ma,

*I am writing to reach you—even if each word I
put down is one word further from where you are.'*

— Ocean Vuong

*for my Mother, Rina*

# Contents

## Mother of Flip-Flops

Mother of flip-flops, of
chipped nail polish on ginger fingers — always
with warm hands, your smile
the largest room in this house where
we kill cockroaches with bay leaf
you boil in your chai.

Mother of the money-plant, of orchids
you cannot take care of, of the garden
overgrown with weeds only you
can't seem to stand, mother
of turning the light on, the switch clicks
in your broken English —

*fill form in, look this apartment*
*what this email say?* — And maybe
before teaching you how to
pronounce f u *r* l *ou* gh i'll
write to Barclays about your
loan, put it in that white pre-

paid envelope but maybe
i won't. Maybe i'll
request a renewal, another chance
to go to school, learn to love stories,
knead out words, to go flirt,

go flirt just a little
more, ride on the back of some
handsome's bike, to keep dancing,
to never be pregnant, to learn to make tarkari

later on in life, for yourself.

     Mother of

learning too early to be a mother

Mother of curries

     i'll also request some dirt for your knees
those black knees of playing

       too late in the streets —

# Time Travel to Moon Festival
*After Sharon Olds*

i have learned to go back
walk around feeling walls,
my forehead wobbling
with bumps, and find that moon
so close so large next to the roof,
where we've left
our bed. it is hot,

the pale pink bricks
too warm to step
on. i think we forget
it ever rained, but the moss
of my childhood home
now blends into
the black sea of a power-

cut. everybody
forgets to breathe
when the electric dies
and nothing is silent.
not the sticky voices
of people watching
the moon from their roofs,

not the cry of a motorbike,
not the fading static
of a Hindi serial.
just one of those nights
rice has been left out

to cook in the driveway
and i am there, like a shy sound,

so dark blue and clumsy
the way my mother rolls out
of bed without noise
getting into a tempo
to look for her husband —
her skin darker, her cheeks
younger, hair blacker and long.

## in the hours of a power cut

even fruit flies singing
their monsoon night-song
cry for their mothers

## On Cowley Road,

the sky is an aubergine —

snow falls from her lilac mouth.
                    Every
flake a bloom of icy feathers,
a morning flight
to
Nepal,
riding the clouds across the Himalayas


their blades,
cutting into
sunlight

*

*remember*
being boys in those mountains, plucking
green coffee beans with the corner of our lips the teeth
peeling thick skin, their
bitter juice cooks into our gums

*remember*
running fingers through blankets of
sun-roasted rice, how our small palms
tried to grab as much as they
could — *how we would sound like burning* —

*remember*
the giggle of naughty fingers poked into bronze pots
filled with fermented wine, the pop of the tongue as

the sweet was sucked from the trail of our index and
we became the world moving around

*remember*
dipping our feet in a stream,
dirt peeled from the gaps of our
toes, washing into the summers
of chasing without breathing

\*

there,
the sound of my name
on my mother's tongue, was the ripple
of water against the pebbles
Here, the sound of my name
is a breeze's shivered press
on a winter puddle
that waits for another boy,
in a pair of black wellies, to run and
shatter

\*

Here, we wander, with lighthouse eyes, trying to peer
through the fog.

                        a street with boneless
                                bodies and traffic lights, where
                        the ping pong tables sit in front of the
                                mosque, where two trench-coated
                        strangers, pigeon-coated, meet

at a bus stop with a single
lamppost between
them to shape out their faces —


I know Cowley Road with all her taste,
of chicken skin in olive oil,
dancing with burnt spices. This perfume rises
from the windows of the Bengali restaurant
 — their indigo lettering, the Mexican place
with its clay walls and silver roof — the rain
here will, in spring, make tin music. There
are the Christian girls in silver boots
cutting dumplings with steam
kisses. The boys in yellow coats.
Their mothers with their paper bags,
smelling of marigold, and turmeric. Bright
hijabs with hummingbirds. Ladhus
and Jalebis with the coating of golden sugar. Then
there are the tokens from
Nepal
the dusk-caught cloth of saris,
the triangular red flag, and
radishes outside in the stalls with
coriander, cucumber,
chilies, tangerines, all barred like animals,
breathing in the arctic air,
sitting homeless,
staring out

                                    into the beds of snow.

## Inheritance
*After Sophie Dunsby*

*first — you learn that you will never be your Father or
your Mother*

&

you will never inherit the hot black kiss of an iron pressed
on your

mother's thigh the brand of her marriage she always hid
behind her lungi

you will never learn how the fabric tightened to her waist

was her way of folding new flesh no longer white no
longer pale

&

you will never inherit her poor courage stealing green
mangoes

from the hospitals with Nepalese writing you can no
longer read

you will never learn that she ran differently then her whole

body giggling mangoes to her chest shaking with breath

&

you will never inherit her one dress bought by her Mother

collecting bottles for rupess she hid inside her bones afraid
of liquor hands

you will never learn that there is a thirst that makes
Fathers thieves

why they eat prayers how they rob their children and wives

&

you will never inherit your Mother's need to run

from school afraid of the things she didn't have —

you will never learn that it was those pencils neon
rubbers rulers

she would never forget to buy her son

&

you will never inherit why your Mother no longer ran

you will never learn why she stopped wearing the uniform

she used to share

## Republic of Mackerel

because time is a tuna sandwich
with some pickles and I am tired
today I spoon out mustard sweat.

today the wheels of my belly will bike
my body's cobbled alleyways, I declare
a republic of mackerel and sunflower oil,

where the streets are soy sauce and
the smiles cut as easy as a knife into tofu. here,
our manifesto is the ugly lover who

will try to make a stir fry out of me, eat
jasmine rice on the side, chew every grain like pieces
of a love song in a foreign language

## Mirror

Fleshy morning breath catches
under the skin of my gums.
The new tooth has started
to peek through. But where is
the wisdom? I thought it
would grow, like pubes, on its own.
Can it bloom here in the overfilled
laundry basket, like a rare
muscular orchid that smells of socks?
I've forgotten how to swallow.
I wash down rice, bread, even honey
with tea. Everyone is laughing
a step ahead of me, and my jokes are
syncopated now, and maybe I
have some form of hay fever among
the other things I've diagnosed
from Healthline: *'how to treat*
*plantar fasciitis'*, the *'symptoms of GERD'*,
the *'benefits of meditating'*, *'how to*
*get a fly out of your ear canal'*, or where
to buy the inhaler to relieve 100 days
stuck in a room filled only with
my own breath.

# Instead

of you leaving, why don't we talk
for a little longer in my room which wouldn't
stink of leftover laundry or footprints
two days dry. We'll laugh like running

water about having no more clean underwear,
or how ridiculous it is that as old as I
am, you'll still buy me those neon pink
pair with the dirty Santa, &

instead of you spreading Vicks on my
chest & fever, we'll burp a cold
drink like we did on summer nights
gossiping with onion and coke still fizzing

on our tongues. Let's try not to forget
the lemon or ice. Instead of you
waiting by the black gate with your Sainsbury's
bag, carrying some dish you rushed into

tupperware afraid of the minutes we might
lose, let's chat shit over chicken
curries with rice, just vaat & tarkari, on plates
cut into banana leaves. We'll giggle

the way we should when I tell you about
the boy who sat on the carpet with me, his
smile so close I could smell the cigarette
off his collar. & you

tell me about your encounters in the
club, how my father is unfortunately
still alive, maybe the latest bus driver you're
crushing on, or perhaps just your day

## boys smell

mother
> your palm on my fever returns me
>> to our old house

to the smell of *boy* moulting pubes *boy* plucking armpits
in handfuls *boy* shaving off the queer *boy* days without a
shower *boy* dripping grease brylcreem *boy* learning to stop
being *boy* shedding & stinking like *boy*

> *fat asian boy*

>> sweating late summers
behind the barracks the suburbs laughing as *fat nepali boy* pants
behind his father on a bicycle *for eating five too many packets*
*of maggis*

back to that
> army house so full
with a soldier's rage there was no room for furniture no love for
the chemical mother returning after scrubbing toilets *boy*
dancing in flesh with the lights out to the hum of the radiator
still white in the dark

## where all the Nepalese gay boys at
*after José Olivarez*

to shame your family is to cut your mother's nose, so
all the Nepalese gay boys are adrift in a world where

Asian mothers sport cocktail dresses on ladies' night
with the tips of their noses missing, knowing we exist

in the unspoken shame of every dinner where *'disowned'*
is passed hand to hand like second servings of tarkari,

where our years-old guilt takes the shape of exams we failed,
or cheated on or failed to cheat on. we live in these rooms

where thanking is harder than telling your parents you
love them but we've learned to walk into every room

like one of our own tired mothers, and yell with a voice
that keeps the dinner warm: *where all the Nepalese gay boys at?*

We've been raised to know how to make all the sound
without a noise, dance to anything with pyar, love, or maya,

to be handsome heroes, sing love loud enough
to make the door frames shake

## Mango Sorbet

Boys

the sweat soaking through our thin white tees
is an open mouth at our armpits asking:

Oh don't we stink of running
Oh don't we stink of crushed nocturnal insects
Oh don't we stink of moonlight whipped across our faces
Oh don't we stink of clothes dripping Mango Sorbet
Oh don't we stink of growing pubes
Oh don't we stink of our horny fat bodies

sticky with love.

## The Cleaners
*My Mother Rina Limbu, and the Housekeepers of Malmaison,
And the World.*


HONEYMOON SUITE

WE ARE THE CLEANERS eating dust     we pick up
dead skin in lumps along the inch of our fingers
        the scent of leftover breakfast pastries on our uniform
rub against our moist armpits like washboards     we reach
up to spread the sheets out wide                 like the
outside sky shaking out their dirty stars


                    sometimes we find the plum mark of lips
on the pillows and   we think this is a woman who has
kissed more than a single lip  this is a woman with hips that
streamline the breeze unlike us         our hips are spiked by
the elbows of chairs unlike us our skin so salty  yes this is a
woman whose skin will taste of lychee  and


                        we are the cleaners who
pour a pint of milk down the cold bowl of the toilet  the
plopping of water on water sounding like clucking   a
drumbeat       we scrub that curved white throat we scrub
until we can see our eyes             until we see our tea
stained faces until we see we are not smiling  then we close
this mouth


ROOM 207 (VIP Suite)

HERE WE REMEMBER
how hungry we are

how back home in the morning we ground poppadum
salt into rice we remember vaat khanu parcha
and rice are the golden tears of the earth

how when we first arrived we would eat what our
husbands got for us how spit split our tongues
how we did not know we were eating our god

how we used to sweep floors holding our lungis
to our waist now we wear Suitable Trousers without
slippers squelching like slaps on hot pavement

we remember that this will be the furthest distance we will
all travel
that the rain at 4am used to sing differently

that we have forgotten to taste with our hands


ROOM 123

PATTING THE PILLOWS
we dream of our boys the ones we left behind          we
dream our boys kissing the picture of their mothers every
night before sleep          we dream they're old enough
to know whether the oranges from the mountains are sweet
or sour          we dream our sons thick with platinum arms
and shins lassoing the moon across the oceans shooting an
arrow at the Sun          we dream the Sun falling
we dream of them catching pockets of light
we dream of them catching a bird in flight then

we dream them men in sunglasses straw sandals melting
into the street  motorbikes growling waiting to carry a girl
through grey rusting gates


## ~~DUMPSTER~~

## TAKING THE BINS OUTSIDE
*We will remember what we always said to our little girls*
*You should eat the leaf*
*You should eat the fruit*
*But not the entire tree*


## ~~ROOM~~ 303

## WE ARE THE CLEANERS MOURNING
our daughters who always knew if
the lids were left too loose the ants would get in

We see our daughters visiting neon hotels for single nights
in the arms of a wobbly man

We see our daughter in her loose check shirt skipping down
the stairs her neck bare against the wind, her arms rustling
branches


We see her head bopping to the breeze forgetting that
nodding
does not mean *please   we will   please don't hit us*

# WE ARE THE CLEANERS

using the trunk of the hoover for each corner and the floor
we are on our hands and knees and we are not even praying

one side of our face  will always  be itchy we become
ants staring into darkness under the beds

some of us  are too old for our backs  to arch
 if  one of us  is running behind  we will come together

and pull together in four directions we will crouch around
like the wives of Krishna, this room a harem, this bed


 our husband

## my grandfather never told us stories

about being a father. mother says look
for them in photos of the homecoming Gurkha
with his sons, hair oiled and shirts ironed; shoes neon
clean new — gifts from white man's country — and imagine
how much they cost him. more than

dinner. more than his children's language,
more than the stories he never knew, how his son
ran away from school, how he climbed over gates
in those same western trainers, took the bus
from Kathmandu to his neighbourhood.

my father laughs as he tells us again how he spat
in the air to look for the right way home.

## boju says

he is now the   2am ambak
      falling on our tin roof &   *maybe*
but i don't have
      words for my grandmother
singing for the ghost   of her husband

still limping around his home
      of pepper trees   monkeys   built   from

   ~~fighting~~ fighting
for the white man — the dead Gurkha

  & his kukri  who once  learned to swim
  with only a word   to stay afloat

                     bhaduri[1]


when someone dies my
mother says even   the fruit-flies sing at   the
funeral
they dance in   between   hot
rain   & grief   &
     laughter of   the neighbourhood
gambling in the   living

------

[1] *courage* / a dead grandfather's middle name / more than courage /

    the पूर्ण bahadur / the absolute courage / something to pass
    on / something he could never pass on

room    telling stories-standing guard — that many   bodies
     will keep   this                 spirit²   away.   & the
family in mourning
must ~~hide~~              away                        touch
no skin taste no salt sleep on hay
call my grandfather's name above


a fire    invite   beg him
 to enter his room once


again


---

² maybe baje is now a song among the slow
   monsoon still whispering to make the lychees
   shiver, fall from the tree into my palms once
   rubbed with his snot an old-grandfathers
   remedy for nettles, the same palms once fat
   taught to slingshot stones like a full stop

## The Cleaner's Wedding

room 214: the Cleaner wearing
      a veil of dust pokes her finger into a
ring left by some woman with plum
      painted nails and graphite earrings.
Beaming like the rim of an eclipse,
      this cut out smooth moon brings out the lilac of

the Cleaner's itchy dress, dirty and coughing
      from hoovering. *'Oh!'* She looks around
the room and thanks the well-kept
      guests for attending her ceremony. She shakes
hands with the Curtains, and thanks him
      for hiding the wilting clouds of this evening.

This thick dusk breaking through the shower
      frame is her bridesmaid, who begins the work
of bending light into marigolds and sunflowers
      sticking them all through the Cleaner's palms as
mehndi. The Cleaner dips these hands in
      orange peels and tomatoes soft from the night before.

She double knots them in little black bins —
      her dowry. As the music begins
the Cleaner mops down the aisle. With arms
      around her groom's grey plastic spine, they
start to sway to a dance she never
      danced. They move

like Autumn rain, Twirl to the Duvet rustling,
      Dip to electric buzzing, Pirouette to the toilet
flushing, and step to the rhythm of 'How is

your son?'— Only to stop. The distant heels
approaching.
The Cleaner drops her husband, abandons
           her ring on the nightstand, and rushes to the
bathroom sink.

There, in her reflection she looks at the trenches
           around her eyes. These are dried up smiles, she thinks,
the mark of a woman with a thousand
           laughters. With her veil worn tight
the Cleaner dreams of what she will cook for dinner
           tonight?

## Grown-ups

The day I run out of words for
how easy and difficult it is to hear

myself speak at dinner, I tell stories
that aren't mine, about the things my mother

believes — that if you are good at cards
you are unlucky in love, to always

pray for the light when it enters
a room, flush the toilet after a bad

dream, or you hiccup
when someone thinks

of you — lately I hold on to this like some
morning prayer. Maybe I'll take

it with me on a run by the meadows
avoiding the geese, or on an evening bike

ride listening to bats for the first
time, squinting at Venus. I tell the sky

it is better to hold hands with these
superstitions than with a man too

drunk to take me to school, believing
that without a scooter there is

nothing a father can teach a son
who has learned to walk all alone

like a grown up.

# Acknowledgements

Thank you to the Out-Spoken Press team for this opportunity to be published and for believing in my words. A huge HUGE thank you to Wayne Holloway-Smith for his patience, for completely backing me, and for taking the time to work on these poems with me.

Thank you to the editors of *The Kindling Journal*, T*he Isis Magazine*, *Unmute* and *Nascent Vol. 1* (Out-spoken Press, 2019), where some of these poems or their earlier versions were first published.

Thanks to Lucy Thynne, Emily Luo, and Natalie Perman for your unconditional support and friendship. To Sophie Dunsby for your constancy and for allowing me to write in response to your poem. To Ocean Vuong, Raymond Antrobus, Mary Jean Chan, Sharon Olds and many more for the endless inspiration.

Thank you to my teachers at Oxford Spires Academy, especially Konni Constantine for getting me places and never letting me lose sight of myself. The biggest and heartiest thanks to my mentor in poetry Kate Clanchy, without whom none of these poems would exist.

Thank you to all my family, particularly my late grandfather Purna Bahadur Subba, and my mother Rina Sunuwar, the source of all my inspiration and love, and to whom I dedicate this pamphlet.

## Other titles by Out-Spoken Press

*Dog Woman* • HELEN QUAH

*Caviar* • SARAH FLETCHER

*Somewhere Something is Burning* • ALICE FRECKNALL

*flinch & air* • LAURA JANE LEE

*Fetch Your Mother's Heart* • LISA LUXX

*Seder* • ADAM KAMMERLING

*54 Questions for the Man Who Sold a Shotgun to My Father*
JOE CARRICK-VARTY

*Lasagne* • WAYNE HOLLOWAY-SMITH

*Mutton Rolls* • ARJI MANUELPILLAI

*Contains Mild Peril* • FRAN LOCK

*Epiphaneia* • RICHARD GEORGES

*Stage Invasion: Poetry & the Spoken Word Renaissance*
PETE BEARDER

*Nascent* • VOL 1: AN ANTHOLOGY

*Ways of Coping* • OLLIE O'NEILL

*The Neighbourhood* • HANNAH LOWE

*The Games* • HARRY JOSEPHINE GILES

*Songs My Enemy Taught Me* • JOELLE TAYLOR

*To Sweeten Bitter* • RAYMOND ANTROBUS

*Dogtooth* • FRAN LOCK

*How You Might Know Me* • SABRINA MAHFOUZ

*Heterogeneous, New & Selected Poems*
ANTHONY ANAXAGOROU

*Titanic* • BRIDGET MINAMORE

Email: press@outspokenldn.com